THIS BOOK BELONGS TO

_____

_____

The New Testament

GALILEE, WHERE JESUS GREW UP, is a hilly area at the heart of which is the Sea of Galilee, a huge freshwater lake. In Jesus' time there were a number of thriving communities, such as Capernaum, Bethsaida, and Tiberias, around the shores of the lake. There were also several important trade routes through the area. This brought the Galileans into contact with people from many countries. Together with other Jewish people from Galilee, Jesus and his family traveled to Jerusalem in Judea for major festivals such as Passover. The long journey, on foot or donkey, would have taken them south along the fertile Jordan valley, avoiding Samaria, to the low-lying area at the north end of the Dead Sea. Jerusalem, in the region of Judea, was the most important Jewish religious center. It was very crowded during Jewish festivals, but it was always busy with merchants traveling there from different parts of the Roman empire.

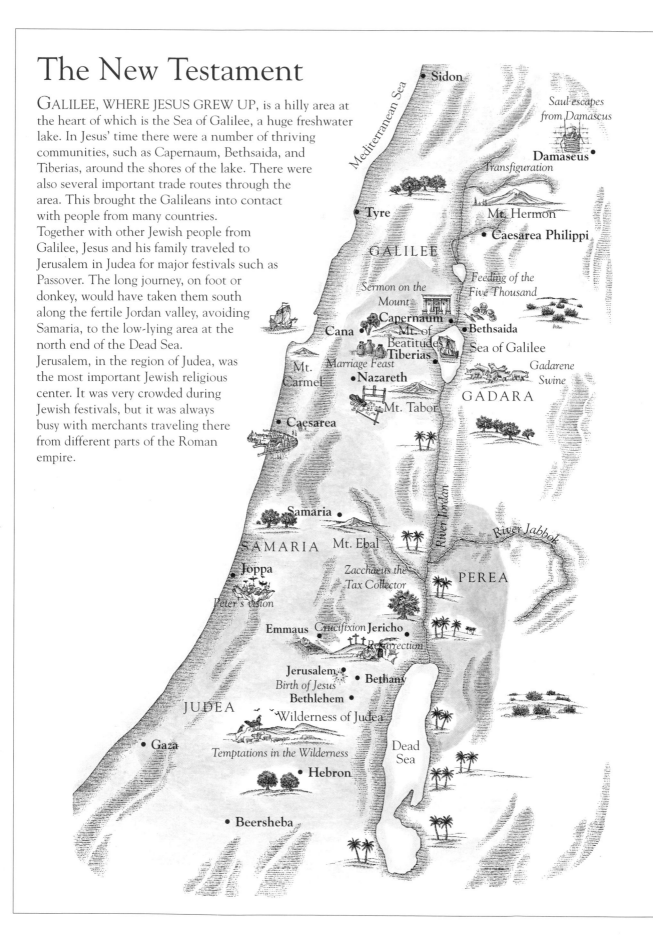

Mediterranean Sea

Sidon

Saul escapes from Damascus

Damascus

Transfiguration

Tyre

Mt. Hermon

Caesarea Philippi

GALILEE

Sermon on the Mount

Feeding of the Five Thousand

Capernaum

Cana

Mt. of Beatitudes

Bethsaida

Sea of Galilee

Tiberias

Gadarene Swine

Mt. Carmel

Marriage Feast

Nazareth

GADARA

Mt. Tabor

Caesarea

Samaria

River Jordan

River Jabbok

SAMARIA

Mt. Ebal

PEREA

Joppa

Zacchaeus the Tax Collector

Peter's vision

Emmaus

Crucifixion

Jericho

Resurrection

Jerusalem

Bethany

Birth of Jesus

Bethlehem

JUDEA

Wilderness of Judea

Gaza

Temptations in the Wilderness

Dead Sea

Hebron

Beersheba

The Miracles of
Jesus

• And other Bible stories •

Retold *by* Selina Hastings

A DK PUBLISHING BOOK

Art Editor Shirley Gwillym
Project Editor Marie Greenwood
Senior Editor Emma Johnson
Designer Sarah Cowley
Additional design by Heather Blackham, Muffy Dodson
Production Ruth Cobb, Marguerite Fenn
Managing Editor Susan Peach
Managing Art Editor Jacquie Gulliver

Introduction and section openers written by
Geoffrey Marshall-Taylor

CONSULTANTS
Educational Consultant
Geoffrey Marshall-Taylor,
Executive Producer, BBC Education,
Responsible for religious radio programmes
for schools

Historical Consultant
Carole Mendleson,
Western Asiatic Department
British Museum, London

Religious Consultants
Reverend Stephen Motyer
London Bible College

Bernadette Chapman and Father Philip Walshe
St Mary's College,
Twickenham

Published in the United States by
DK PUBLISHING, Inc.,
95 Madison Avenue, New York, NY 10016

The Children's Illustrated Bible
Copyright © 1994 Dorling Kindersley Limited, London
Text copyright © 1994 Selina Hastings
The right of Selina Hastings to be identified as the Author
of this Work has been asserted by her in accordance with
the Copyright Designs and Patents Act 1988.

A CIP catalog record for this book is available from the
Library of Congress.

ISBN 07513-5483-X
Reproduced by Colourscan, Singapore
Printed and bound in Spain by Artes Graficas
Toledo S.A.   D.L.TO: 582-1996

Extracts from the Authorised Version of the Bible (The
King James Bible), the rights of which are vested in the
Crown, are reproduced by permission of the Crown's
Patentee, Cambridge University Press.

CONTENTS

Jesus of Galilee   6

The Marriage Feast of Cana   8

Healing the Sick   10

The Centurion's Servant   12

Jesus Calms the Storm   14

The Gadarene Swine   15

Jairus' Daughter   16

The Feeding of the Five Thousand   18

Jesus Walks on the Water   20

The Transfiguration   22

Mary, Martha, and Lazarus   24

Judas Plots to Betray Jesus   26

Preparing for the Passover   28

The Last Supper   30

The Garden of Gethsemane   32

Peter's Denial   34

Jesus Before the Sanhedrin   36

Jesus Before Pilate   38

The Crucifixion   40

The Resurrection   42

On the Road to Emmaus   44

The Ascension   46

Tongues of Fire   48

Peter the Healer   50

Saul's Journey to Damascus   52

Peter and Cornelius   54

Peter in Prison   56

Paul's Journeys   58

Paul Journeys to Rome   60

Index   62

Who's Who in the Bible Stories/
Acknowledgments   64

Jesus of Galilee

JESUS GREW UP IN THE town of Nazareth, in a northern area of Palestine called Galilee. The people there had a reputation for being independent and strong-minded. They spoke with their own accent, which meant that in Jerusalem everybody could tell that Jesus and most of his friends came from Galilee.

Jesus was born in Judea, in the small town of Bethlehem, about 100 miles (160 km) to the south of Nazareth. However, most of the events of his adult life – healing the sick, the miracles, the sermon on the mount – took place in Galilee.

No one knows the exact date of Jesus' birth, but it was probably what we now call 5 or 4 BC, in

The map of Galilee, above right, shows the area in which Jesus grew up and the main places connected with his ministry.

the reign of the Roman emperor, Augustus.

Jesus was brought up by his mother, Mary, and by her husband, Joseph, a carpenter. In their workshop in Nazareth they would have made and mended wooden items such as doors, carts, ladders, tools, and even bowls. They probably traveled around Galilee doing building work.

What was Jesus Like?

Down the centuries artists have shown Jesus in paintings, mosaics, carvings, and stained-glass windows. The way he appeared depended on the idea of Jesus the artists wanted to portray. For example, sometimes they emphasized his strength, sometimes his gentleness. In reality, he probably would have had dark hair and dark eyes. Because of his work as a carpenter, his shoulders would have been broad and his arms strong.

Jesus was Jewish. He and his family went to the synagogue at Nazareth, where each Sabbath (from dusk on Friday to dusk on Saturday) services were held and words were read from the

Torah, the first five books of the Bible. Jesus would have learnt about the rest of the Jewish Bible, what Christians call the Old Testament, together with other important Jewish writings. When he was 12 years old, he impressed the teachers in the temple in Jerusalem by his learning and wisdom.

At the age of 30, Jesus began to attract large crowds who came to hear him teach about God and to see him heal the sick. He mixed with all kinds of people, and could be serious and funny, blunt and kind.

The Son of God

Jesus made enemies because he claimed that he was the Son of God. However, many believed he was the Messiah, the special person whom God had promised to send into the world and whom the Hebrew prophets had predicted would lead Israel to greatness. The death of Jesus is important to Christians because they believe that, in dying, he was showing God's love for all people. For this reason the cross became the main symbol of Christianity. Christians believe, however, that death did not put an end to Jesus, but that his spirit lives on, especially through his followers.

SEA OF GALILEE
Many of the events of Jesus' life took place on the shores and in the towns around the Sea of Galilee. This freshwater lake, set between high hills, is called by several different names in the Bible, including the Lake of Gennesaret, and the Sea of Tiberias.

In Jesus' day, the Sea of Galilee was a rich source of fish. It was on the shores of the lake that Jesus found his first disciples – the fishermen Peter, Andrew, James, and John.

Friends and Followers

The first followers, or disciples, of Jesus were fishermen from Galilee. For three years these 12 men, who came to be known as his apostles, left their homes and jobs to travel with him to teach people about God. They were his close companions.

The first disciples called by Jesus were fishermen.

Three of Jesus' closest friends lived just outside Jerusalem, at Bethany. They were Martha, her sister Mary, and their brother Lazarus. When Jesus was in Jerusalem he often stayed at their house. Jesus had another friend called Mary, who came from Magdala on the western shore of the Sea of Galilee. She had led a life of which people disapproved, but Jesus helped her to make a fresh start. She was devoted to him and when he was crucified, she stayed near his cross with Mary, the mother of Jesus, and Mary, the mother of the disciple James.

There were several women among Jesus' close friends.

Jesus had followers from all walks of life: from tax collectors, such as Matthew, to wealthy, powerful people, such as Joseph of Arimathea, who was a member of the Sanhedrin, the Jewish council. It was Joseph who provided a tomb for Jesus to be buried in. Jesus turned no one away. He even showed compassion to Roman soldiers, who were hated by many for ruling over their land.

Jesus helped people from many different backgrounds.

The Marriage Feast of Cana

WATER JARS
Stone jars, like the ones above, were used for carrying and storing water. The larger jars could hold up to 30 gallons (115 liters).

N THE TOWN OF CANA in Galilee there was a wedding. Jesus and his mother, Mary, were invited, and so were the twelve disciples. The guests were sitting down to the feast when Mary noticed that the jugs were already empty. She whispered to her son, "There is no more wine." She then told a servant who was standing nearby to do whatever Jesus said.

Now standing against the wall were some huge stone water jars, used in the religious rituals of ceremonial washing, each so big that two men were needed to carry it. Jesus beckoned the servant to him. "Fill those jars with water," he told him; and when the jars had been

Mary and the disciples accompany Jesus to the wedding

Mary

bride

Jesus

servant

stone water jars

Jesus tells a servant to fill some stone jars with water and to take them to the guest of honor

filled to the brim, Jesus said, "Now take some to the guest of honor so that he may taste it."

The most important guest, sitting close to the bridegroom, did not know where this wine had come from, but at the first sip he knew it was exceptionally good. Rising to his feet, he drank a toast. "You are a generous man!" he said to the bridegroom. "Most people give good wine at the start of a banquet, then let us get drunk on the poor stuff. But you have kept the best till last!" And he threw his head back and happily swallowed a great mouthful of wine.

The miracle at the wedding in Cana was the first that Jesus worked. In this way he revealed his heavenly glory, and strengthened the disciples' faith in him.

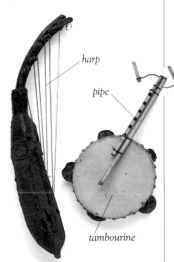

CANA
The town of Cana is traditionally thought to be Kefar Kana, shown above. The town lies in a valley north of Nazareth, in Galilee. It is surrounded by olive and pomegranate trees. Two churches have been built there to commemorate Jesus' miracle.

The guest of honor toasts the bridegroom for keeping the best wine till last

bridegroom

harp

pipe

tambourine

MAKING MUSIC
Musicians often played at Jewish wedding feasts. Harps were usually played with a plectrum, or pick. The musicians would play their pipes and tambourines as the women danced and sang.

Healing the Sick

LEPER
In the Bible, the word "leprosy" stands for a variety of skin diseases. Lepers lived apart from the community to prevent the spreading of infection. They had to wear torn clothes and cry "unclean, unclean" to insure that no one approached them. Yet Jesus was not afraid to touch the leper when he came to him to be cured.

N EWS OF JESUS' TEACHINGS had spread throughout the land, and wherever he went he was followed by vast crowds. One day in Capernaum a leper came up to Jesus, saying, "Lord, if you are willing, you can cure me." Moved by compassion, Jesus reached out his hand and touched him. "I am willing: be clean."

Instantly the man saw that his legs and arms were whole and his skin unmarked. "Go on your way," said Jesus, "Show yourself to a priest: he will offer sacrifices and declare you cured. But tell no one else about what has happened."

But the leper was so overjoyed at being cured that he described the miracle to everyone he met. Soon Jesus was unable to walk down the

Four friends lower an invalid through the roof of the house to be cured by Jesus

Jesus touches the leper and cures him

AND JESUS, MOVED WITH COMPASSION, PUT FORTH HIS HAND, AND TOUCHED HIM AND SAITH UNTO HIM, "I WILL; BE THOU CLEAN."
MARK 1:41

street without being surrounded by dozens of eager followers.

Later, Jesus was preaching in a house so full of people that there was hardly room to breathe. Four men arrived at the house, carrying a stretcher on which lay a man who was completely paralyzed. Realizing that they had no hope of entering by the door, they went up on the roof. There they made a hole, through which they lowered the invalid.

Jesus looked at the man and said, "My son, your sins are forgiven."

But some Pharisees and Jewish leaders overheard these words. Among themselves they accused Jesus of insulting God. They thought this man had no right to take upon himself such authority: only God could forgive sin.

Jesus, knowing what was in their minds, said, "Why do you think badly of me? Do you believe that I do not have the right to forgive sins? Which is easier, to forgive this man's sins, or to make him walk? But so that you will know that I have the power to forgive sins...." Pausing, he turned to the paralyzed man and said, "Get up, take your bed, and go home." Speechless, the man got up at once and returned to his house. The crowds who had seen the miracle talked excitedly and went away praising God. "We have never seen anything like this," they said.

REED-ROOFED HOUSES
In Jesus' time, most Galilean houses had flat roofs, similar to the ones above. The roofs were made from layers of reeds and mud laid on top of wooden beams. The surface was smoothed with a roller.

The man, now cured, takes up his mat and walks home

The crowds go away, praising God

The Pharisees and the Jewish leaders accuse Jesus of insulting God

The Centurion's Servant

Jesus arrives in Capernaum and is met by Jewish elders and teachers

They tell Jesus that the centurion's servant is ill

THE CENTURION ANSWERED AND SAID, "LORD, I AM NOT WORTHY THAT THOU SHOULDST COME UNDER MY ROOF: BUT SPEAK THE WORD ONLY, AND MY SERVANT SHALL BE HEALED."

MATTHEW 8:8

ESUS PREACHED throughout the land for many days until he returned to the city of Capernaum. Here he was met by some Jewish elders, who told him of a man who was lying dangerously ill. He was the much-loved servant of a Roman soldier, a centurion. They told Jesus that the centurion had asked them to beg Jesus to come to him. "This centurion is a good man," said the elders. "He built a synagogue for us, and he has done much to help our people."

But as Jesus approached the house, the centurion himself came out to meet him. "Lord, I thank you for your trouble, but do not come any further. I know I am not fit to stand before you, nor am I worthy to ask you into my house. I am a man used to authority, to giving orders and having them obeyed – and in the same way I know that you have only to say the word, and my servant will be cured."

Jesus tells the centurion that his servant is healed

The elders are amazed when they find that the servant is cured

ROMAN UNIFORM
Centurions were in charge of a troop of Roman soldiers. The soldiers wore sandals with iron hobnails on the soles, which were ideal for marching. They carried short swords, which were easy to wield in battle.

Jesus, astonished at the soldier's speech, turned to the people who were following him. "Look at this man, and listen to what I am about to say. I have not in the whole of Israel found a stronger nor a truer faith." Then to the centurion he said, "Go to your servant, for he is now healed."

The elders were amazed, even more so when they went to the house and found the servant completely cured.

Jesus Calms the Storm

JESUS AND HIS DISCIPLES were on the Sea of Galilee, aboard a small fishing boat. It was evening, and Jesus, tired from preaching all day, fell asleep on some cushions in the stern. Suddenly a violent storm blew up. The sky darkened, the wind howled and gigantic waves crashed over the little vessel.

Frightened, the disciples shook Jesus awake. "Save us, Lord!" they cried. "Our boat will sink, and we shall drown!"

"Why are you afraid?" said Jesus. "Have you no faith?" Stretching his hands out over the lake, he spoke to the wind and the waves: "Peace. Be calm." Instantly the storm died down and the lake grew still.

"How great a man he is," exclaimed the disciples. "Even the wind and the waves obey him!"

HIS DISCIPLES CAME TO HIM, AND AWOKE HIM, SAYING, "LORD, SAVE US: WE PERISH." AND HE SAITH UNTO THEM, "WHY ARE YE FEARFUL, O YE OF LITTLE FAITH?" THEN HE AROSE, AND REBUKED THE WINDS AND THE SEA; AND THERE WAS A GREAT CALM.

MATTHEW 8:25-26

Jesus calls on the wind and waves to be calm

The disciples are frightened in the storm

The Gadarene Swine

AFTER THE STORM, Jesus and the disciples came safely to shore, to the country of the Gadarenes. As they stepped once more onto dry land, a man came running toward them. He was half naked and appeared to be possessed by evil spirits. His hair was long, his eyes wild, and he snapped and snarled like a beast. Many times he had been caught and chained, but he was so strong that each time he had broken free. No one was able to calm him. Now he lived among the tombstones in the surrounding hills, howling and crying day and night, and in his misery cutting himself with sharp stones.

He had seen Jesus from a long way off. "What do you want, Son of God?" he cried out in a loud voice, "Have you come to torment me?"

"What is your name?" Jesus asked.

"My name is Legion," replied the man. "Legion – for there are many demons within me."

Now feeding nearby was a large herd of nearly two thousand pigs. Jesus commanded the demons to leave the man. "Go!" he said. "Leave this man and enter instead the bodies of those pigs!"

So the evil spirits left the man and took possession of the herd of swine. Suddenly the pigs stopped feeding, looked up, and grunting and snorting, galloped to the cliff's edge and hurled themselves into the sea.

The men who were looking after the herd watched in horror as the pigs leapt to their deaths. They turned and ran back to the town to tell their story. A crowd gathered and came back to see for themselves. They were amazed to find the madman now cured of his madness. He was fully clothed, sitting quietly and talking to Jesus. The people were frightened by the extraordinary change in the man and begged Jesus to leave the country.

As Jesus was getting into the boat once more, the man who had been possessed by demons ran toward him. He pleaded with Jesus to let him go with him. Jesus said, "No, it is best that you return home. Tell your friends what the Lord has done, and how he has shown his mercy toward you."

Jesus commands the demons to leave the man and enter a herd of pigs

DEMON
The statue above is of an Assyrian demon. In the Bible, demons are evil spirits that join with the devil to oppose God and humans. In Jesus' time, it was believed that demons entered humans and caused disease and mental illnesses.

Jairus' Daughter

synagogue

As Jesus goes to see Jairus' daughter, a woman touches the hem of Jesus' robe and is cured

Jairus, head of the synagogue, falls to his knees and asks Jesus to cure his daughter

Peter

Jesus

Jairus

SYNAGOGUE
A synagogue is a Jewish place of worship. Above are the ruins of a synagogue in Capernaum. Synagogues probably originated during the Jewish exile in Babylon, when the people were separated from the temple in Jerusalem. Synagogues came to be used as social, as well as religious, centers.

THE HEAD OF THE SYNAGOGUE came to Jesus, and falling on his knees, begged for his help. "My little daughter is dying," he said, weeping. "I implore you to lay your hands on her and make her well!"

As Jesus left with the man, a woman made her way through the crowd and timidly felt the hem of his robe. For twelve years she had suffered from internal bleeding, which no doctor could cure. She knew that Jesus would heal her, if she could only touch him.

Jesus stopped, and turned around. "Who touched me?" he asked.

Peter was puzzled by Jesus' question. "In such a crush of people," he said, "you ask who touched you?"

But Jesus looked straight at the woman, who shrank back trembling. "Do not be afraid, my daughter," he said. "Your faith in God has cured you. Go in peace, and be free from suffering." And from that moment the woman was well.

When Jesus reached the house where the young girl lay, he saw people wailing and wringing their hands, and pipers playing music for the dead. "Why do you come here?" they asked Jesus. "She is dead: there is nothing you can do."

"The girl is not dead: she is sleeping." said Jesus. No one believed him, and some laughed scornfully at his words. He went into the house, allowing only Peter, James, and John to come with him.

Jesus stood with the girl's mother and father beside the child. Gently taking her hand, he said, "Little girl, get up from your bed." The child opened her eyes, and as naturally as if she had indeed been asleep, got up from her bed, and hugged both her parents.

"Now give her something to eat," Jesus said to them. "But tell no one what has taken place in this room."

MOURNING SOUNDS
In Jesus' time, Jewish people used music to express sorrow as well as joy. The reed pipe had a sad, wailing tone and was often played at times of mourning, as at the death of Jairus' daughter.

Peter, James, and John enter Jairus' house

Peter   James   John

The girl's mother and father weep by her bed

Pipers play and people wail and wring their hands, as Jairus' daughter lies dead

Jesus gently takes the girl by the hand and she sits up, alive and well

The Feeding of the Five Thousand

Jesus and his disciples cross the Sea of Galilee by boat

THEN HE TOOK THE FIVE LOAVES AND THE TWO FISHES, AND LOOKING UP TO HEAVEN, HE BLESSED THEM, AND BRAKE, AND GAVE TO THE DISCIPLES TO SET BEFORE THE MULTITUDE. AND THEY DID EAT, AND WERE ALL FILLED.
LUKE 9:16-17

LOAVES AND FISHES
The crowds were fed with unleavened bread made from barley. Barley was a common crop in Palestine because it could grow in poor soil. The fish would have been salted to preserve them.

ESUS WISHED TO SPEND A LITTLE TIME away from the crowds, so he, along with his twelve disciples, went by boat across the Sea of Galilee to a quiet desert region near Bethsaida. However, it soon became known where he was going, and thousands of people poured out of towns and cities to meet him there. When Jesus saw how greatly they needed him, he was moved, and walked among the crowd, talking, answering questions, and healing those who were ill.

Toward evening the disciples said, "Surely it is time for you to send these crowds away? You are tired and need to rest. Let them look after themselves, and find food where they can."

"No," said Jesus. "There is no need for them to go. And you can feed them here."

"But there are more than five thousand people!" exclaimed the disciples.

Then Andrew, the brother of Simon, said, "There is a boy here who has five loaves of barley bread and two small fish, but what use is so little divided among so many?"

Jesus told everyone to sit down on the grass, then he took the bread and the two fish from the boy, and blessed them. He told his disciples to give food to every man, woman, and child present. The disciples did as he asked them, and were astonished to find not only that there was plenty for all, but that afterward twelve baskets were filled with the food that remained.

A boy approaches Jesus carrying a basket of five loaves and two fish

The disciples give the food to all the people

Twelve baskets full of food are left over

Jesus Walks on the Water

JESUS TOLD HIS DISCIPLES to go ahead of him by boat across the Sea of Galilee, while he sent away the crowds that had come to hear him. When everyone had gone, Jesus went a little way up the mountain to pray by himself.

That evening a strong wind began to blow, and the boat carrying the disciples was tossed and buffeted by the waves. The harder they struggled to row toward shore, the more swiftly their little boat was swept off course. Knowing they were in distress, Jesus went to them, walking on the surface of the water. As they saw him approach through the dark, they thought he was a ghost, and cried out in fear.

Jesus goes up the mountain to pray by himself

The boat carrying the disciples is tossed and buffeted by the waves

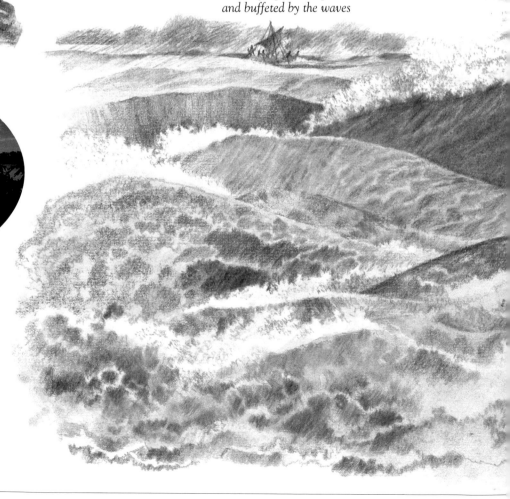

SEA OF GALILEE
The Sea of Galilee is a large, freshwater lake that is fed by the River Jordan. It is about 13 miles (21 km) long and reaches a width of 8 miles (13 km). The lake is known for its sudden fierce winds and violent storms. When Jesus walked on the lake and calmed the storm, it was a sign of his control over nature.

"It is I," he said. "Do not be afraid."

"If it is you, Lord," said Peter, "let me walk to you on the water."

"Come," said Jesus.

Jumping over the side, Peter took several steps across the surface of the lake, but when he looked down at the swirling waves, his courage failed him, and he began to sink. "Save me, Lord!" he cried.

Jesus stretched out his hands and held on to him. "Why do you not have faith?" he asked. Then he went with Peter into the boat. At once, the wind died down, and the water grew calm. The disciples, filled with awe, said to Jesus, "Truly, you are the son of God."

IMMEDIATELY JESUS STRETCHED FORTH HIS HAND, AND CAUGHT HIM, AND SAID UNTO HIM, "O THOU OF LITTLE FAITH, WHEREFORE DIDST THOU DOUBT?"
MATTHEW 14:31

The disciples' boat is swept off course

Peter begins to sink as he walks on the water toward Jesus

Jesus, walking on the surface of the water, stretches out his hands to help Peter

The Transfiguration

Jesus tells Peter that he will give him the keys of God's kingdom

PETER THE LEADER
This mosaic shows Peter, whose name means "rock." When Jesus said that he would give Peter the keys to the kingdom, he meant that Peter was to take a leading role in the church.

HAVING REACHED CAESAREA PHILIPPI, Jesus began to talk to his disciples. "Who do people say I am?" he asked them.

"Some say you are John the Baptist, others that you are one of the prophets, Jeremiah or Elijah," they told him.

"Who do you say that I am?"

"You are Christ, the son of God," Peter replied.

"You, Peter, are blessed, for God himself has revealed this to you. On you, as on a rock, I shall build my church, and to you will I give the keys of the kingdom of Heaven."

Then Jesus explained to his disciples that they must tell no one of his true identity. "The time will soon come when I must go to Jerusalem, and there I shall suffer at the hands of the chief priests and officers of the law. I shall be tried, condemned, and executed, but on the third day after my death, I shall rise again."

"This shall not happen to you!" Peter exclaimed. "It must never happen!"

"Do not deny the will of God. You are thinking of your own wishes, instead of God's."

Then Jesus said to his disciples, "Those who wish to follow me must, for my sake, give up all the comforts and riches of this life, but their reward in Heaven will be great. What are great possessions worth if, to win them, a man forfeits his soul and the chance of eternal happiness?"

A week later, Jesus took Peter, James, and John, the brother of James, up on a high mountain to pray. Suddenly the three men saw the appearance of Jesus change: his face shone like the sun and his clothes were as white as the purest snow. Then Moses and Elijah appeared and talked to Jesus. The disciples were terrified, and Peter, unsure what to do, said, "Lord, it is wonderful that we are all here. Let us put up three tents, one for you, one for Moses, and one for Elijah."

Then a bright cloud passed over, and the voice of God was heard, saying "This is my son, with whom I am well pleased. Listen to him."

The disciples fell on the ground in fear, covering their eyes. Jesus came to them and touched each on the shoulder. "Do not be afraid," he said. Timidly, they looked up, but saw only Jesus standing before them.

As they came down the mountain, Jesus said, "Tell no one what you have seen until after I have died and risen from the dead."

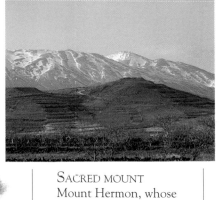

Jesus' appearance changes and Moses and Elijah appear next to him

Elijah

Moses

John

James

Peter

Peter, James, and John hide their faces in fear

SACRED MOUNT
Mount Hermon, whose name means "sacred mountain," lies near Caesarea Philippi and is the most likely site of the transfiguration of Jesus. The snow-covered peaks reach a height of over 9,000 feet (2,700 m). When Jesus was transfigured, the glory of God shone through him and he was revealed as the son of God. Beside him were Moses, representing Jewish law, and Elijah, representing the prophets. This was to show that Jesus fulfilled the words of the law and the prophets.

BEHOLD, A BRIGHT CLOUD OVERSHADOWED THEM: AND BEHOLD A VOICE OUT OF THE CLOUD, WHICH SAID, "THIS IS MY BELOVED SON, IN WHOM I AM WELL PLEASED; HEAR YE HIM."
MATTHEW 17:5

Mary, Martha, and Lazarus

ESUS ARRIVED IN A VILLAGE CALLED BETHANY, not far from Jerusalem, and was invited to the house of Mary and Martha, who were sisters. Mary sat at Jesus' feet listening as he talked, while Martha hurried to and fro preparing the food. After a while she began to resent the fact that her sister was doing nothing to help. "It is not right, Lord, that Mary should sit at your feet, while I do all the work," she complained.

"But Mary is wise," he gently told her. "It is more important to listen to my teaching, as she does, than to worry, like you, about the affairs of the house."

The two sisters had a brother called Lazarus, and a little while after Jesus had left, Lazarus fell seriously ill. Mary and Martha sent word to Jesus, begging him to come and save their brother's life.

The message reached Jesus as he was talking to his disciples. "Lazarus is sleeping," he said. "I will go and awaken him." But he remained where he was for several days before returning to Bethany.

As he approached the sisters' house, Martha, in tears, ran out to meet him. "If only you had been here, Lord, my brother would not have died!"

"Your brother shall rise from death. You must have faith and believe

JESUS ANSWERED AND SAID UNTO HER, "MARTHA, MARTHA, THOU ART CAREFUL AND TROUBLED ABOUT MANY THINGS: BUT ONE THING IS NEEDFUL; AND MARY HATH CHOSEN THAT GOOD PART, WHICH SHALL NOT BE TAKEN AWAY FROM HER."
LUKE 10:41-42

Martha works hard preparing the food

Jesus tells Martha not to worry about her work, but to listen to him, as Mary is doing

Jesus listens as Martha tells him that her brother, Lazarus, is dead

what I have taught you of the resurrection of the dead."

Mary, too, came out to Jesus, weeping as if her heart would break. When he saw the strength of her grief, he was deeply moved. "Where has Lazarus been laid?" he asked her. Accompanied by mourning relations, she led him to the tomb, which was in a cave, its mouth sealed by a heavy stone.

"Take away the stone," said Jesus. With difficulty, the stone was rolled to one side.

"Lazarus, arise!" To everyone's astonishment, Lazarus, his head and body covered in the white linen of his shroud, walked out of the cave. It was as Jesus had said: the dead man had been brought back to life, as if simply awakened from sleep.

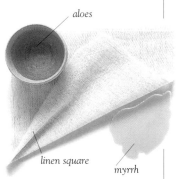

aloes

linen square

myrrh

BURIAL

According to Jewish tradition, burials usually took place on the day of death. The body was washed then wrapped in a linen cloth. A linen square was wrapped around the head. Aloes and myrrh were often placed between the folds of linen. Myrrh was an expensive and fragrant gum from the bark of a tree. Aloes was juice from a medicinal plant.

Lazarus walks out of the cave at Jesus' bidding

Judas Plots to Betray Jesus

SPIKENARD
The spikenard, or ointment, that Mary used to anoint Jesus came from the fragrant oil produced by the dried roots and stems of the spikenard plant. The plant grows in the Himalayas in India.

PRECIOUS GIFT
Spikenard was imported from India into Palestine in alabaster jars, such as the one above. When Mary broke the jar and anointed Jesus with the valuable ointment, it was to honor him as a special guest. Spikenard was also used to anoint bodies before burial.

Martha serves dinner to Jesus and his disciples

Martha

Lazarus

Jesus

Mary

Mary pours precious spikenard over Jesus' feet, then wipes them clean with her hair

Judas is shocked that Mary used such expensive ointment

I T WAS SIX DAYS before the festival of Passover. Jesus and his disciples had traveled to Bethany, which lay just outside Jerusalem. They went to stay at the house of Jesus' friends, Mary, Martha, and their brother Lazarus, whom Jesus had earlier raised from the dead.

Martha made them very welcome and prepared a dinner in Jesus' honor. Jesus and his disciples sat down to the feast and Martha busily served them. Then Mary came up to Jesus, carrying an alabaster jar of precious spikenard. She broke the jar and gently rubbed his feet with the soothing ointment, afterward wiping them clean with her hair. Soon the whole house was filled with the spikenard's sweet-smelling perfume.

Judas Iscariot, one of the twelve disciples, was shocked that Mary should have used something so expensive. "You could have sold that ointment for a good sum and given the money to the poor! It is worth about the same as a year's wage to a laborer," he said to her angrily.

"Leave her alone," said Jesus. "She has done a beautiful thing for me. The poor you will always have with you, but you will not always have me with you. By anointing me with this perfume, she is preparing me for the day of my burial. What she has done will always be remembered."

Meanwhile the priests, scribes, and elders, who were members of the Jewish council, the Sanhedrin, assembled at the house of Caiaphas, the high priest. They were looking for an excuse to arrest Jesus and execute him, for they were afraid of his influence with the people. Judas went to them in secret and discussed with them how he might betray Jesus.

"What will you give me if I deliver Jesus into your hands?" he asked them.

"Thirty pieces of silver."
Judas agreed to this, and Caiaphas counted the thirty coins into his hand, one by one.

From then on Judas never left Jesus' side, watching and waiting for his opportunity to hand him over to the Jewish council.

THEN ONE OF THE TWELVE, CALLED JUDAS ISCARIOT, WENT UNTO THE CHIEF PRIESTS, AND SAID UNTO THEM, "WHAT WILL YE GIVE ME, AND I WILL DELIVER HIM UNTO YOU?" AND THEY CONVENANTED WITH HIM FOR THIRTY PIECES OF SILVER.
MATTHEW 26:14-15

Judas agrees to deliver Jesus into Caiaphas' hands for thirty pieces of silver

Preparing for the Passover

Peter and John follow a man carrying a jar of water

The man leads them to a certain house

Peter and John ask the owner of the house to show them the upstairs room where they are to celebrate Passover

UPPER ROOM
The site of the "upper room" is traditionally believed to be the Coenaculum, or "dining room," on Mount Zion in Jerusalem. Wealthy people often set aside their upstairs room for entertaining guests.

IT WAS A FEW DAYS before Passover, and Jesus knew that the time was near when he would leave this world and the people he loved, and join God in Heaven.

The disciples came to him to ask where they should prepare the Passover meal. Jesus told Peter and John to go into Jerusalem. "There you will see a man carrying a jar of water. Follow him, and speak to the owner of the house to which he goes. Ask him to show you the room in which your teacher will celebrate Passover with his disciples. He will take you to a large upstairs room, which will have in it everything you need. There you will stay and prepare for the feast."

The two men did exactly as Jesus told them, and when everything was ready, Jesus and the rest of the disciples arrived at the house and went into the room upstairs.

Jesus then took off his outer robe, and wrapped a towel around his waist. He poured water into a bowl and then knelt in front of each of the twelve disciples, washing their feet and drying them with his towel. But when it was Peter's turn, he objected. "Why do you do this, Lord?" he asked. "I cannot allow you to kneel and wash my feet."

Jesus said, "If you do not let me wash your feet, then you will not be part of me."

"Then, Lord, wash not only my feet, but my hands and my head as well!" said Peter.

When he had finished, Jesus put on his robe and sat down. "Now that I, your Lord, have washed your feet, you should wash one another's feet. I have set you an example, that you may learn that all of you are equal, that the master is not greater than his servant, and that you should behave humbly and kindly toward each other."

FOOT BATH
In Jesus' time it was the custom for people to have the dust washed from their feet on entering a house. It was a task usually performed by servants. When Jesus washed the disciples' feet he was teaching them to serve one another, just as he served them.

The disciples gather together in the upstairs room

Jesus washes the feet of each of the disciples

Peter does not want Jesus to wash his feet

The Last Supper

*Jesus blesses the bread, breaks it,
and gives it to his disciples*

AND AS THEY DID EAT, JESUS TOOK BREAD, AND BLESSED, AND BRAKE IT, AND GAVE TO THEM, AND SAID, "TAKE, EAT; THIS IS MY BODY." AND HE TOOK THE CUP, AND WHEN HE HAD GIVEN THANKS, HE GAVE IT TO THEM: AND THEY ALL DRANK OF IT.

MARK 14:22-23

*The disciples are horrified when
Jesus says that one of them
will betray him*

BREAD AND WINE
When Jesus shared the Passover bread and wine with his disciples he surprised them by making them picture his body and his blood. Today, Christians eat and drink in memory of Christ's death.

JESUS AND HIS DISCIPLES were reclining at their Passover meal. Jesus blessed the matzoh bread and broke it, saying to them, "Take this and eat it, for it is my body."

Then he blessed the wine and passed around his cup. "Drink this, for this is my blood."

Then Jesus looked at each man in turn, his face full of sorrow. "One of you sitting here will betray me."

The disciples were horrified, and looked at each other in dismay. "Is it you?" they asked each other. "Is it him? Is it me?"

Judas leaves the room and walks out into the night

JOHN
The disciple who sat near Jesus during the meal is described in John's gospel as "the man whom Jesus loved." This may have been John himself.

Peter whispered to the disciple who was sitting next to Jesus, "Ask the Master which one he means." This disciple, whom Jesus loved dearly, leaned toward him and asked, "Lord, which one of us is it?"

"The one to whom I shall give this bread," replied Jesus. Then he took a piece from the loaf, dipped it in the dish in front of him, and handed it to Judas Iscariot. "Do whatever you have to do," said Jesus, "but do it quickly."

With a start, Judas got up from the table, left the room, and walked out into the night.

The Garden of Gethsemane

ESUS AND HIS DISCIPLES walked to a garden called Gethsemane, a quiet place they knew and loved on the Mount of Olives. "Stay here for a little while," said Jesus, "while I go and pray." He took with him Peter, James, and John. "My heart is full of sadness," he told them. "Keep watch over me while I pray."

MOUNT OF OLIVES
The Mount of Olives lies to the east of Jerusalem, across from the site of Herod's Temple, where the Dome of the Rock now stands. Jesus showed his human side when he came to the Mount of Olives to pray, and struggled to come to terms with his approaching death.

OLIVE GROVE
Olive trees have a long life and can produce fruit for hundreds of years. The Garden of Gethsemane lay in an olive grove on the Mount of Olives, but the exact site is not known.

Peter, James, and John fall asleep while Jesus is praying

Jesus, full of grief, prays to God

Jesus moved a little farther off, where he lay down in prayer, his face to the ground in an agony of grief.

"Father, please take this cup of suffering from me. But I will always obey you. Let your will, not mine, be done."

He returned to the three men, only to find them fast asleep. "Could you not stay awake for just one hour?" he said. "Please keep watch while I pray." Again he went away to pray, and again the disciples fell asleep, for their eyes were heavy. A third time this happened, then Jesus said, "No matter: the hour has come. The traitor is here!"

As he spoke, Judas arrived, followed by a large number of men sent by the high priest, all armed with swords and clubs and carrying burning torches. Judas went up to Jesus and kissed him on the cheek. This was the prearranged signal. Immediately, two men seized Jesus and held him tightly. At once Peter drew his sword and struck off the ear of one of the guards. But Jesus rebuked him. "Put away your sword," he said. "If I need protection, it is my Father in Heaven who will protect me." He touched the man, and at once his ear was whole.

The disciples, terrified at what they saw happening, turned and ran for their lives. Among the crowd was a young man dressed only in a strip of linen. Armed soldiers tried to arrest him, but although they caught hold of his garment, he slipped from them and ran away naked.

MARK
In Mark's Gospel, a man runs away naked when Jesus is arrested. Scholars have suggested that the man may have been Mark himself, as only Mark tells this story.

A young man runs away naked

Soldiers come to arrest Jesus

Peter draws his sword and strikes off the ear of one of the guards

Judas kisses Jesus on the cheek as a signal to the guards to arrest him

Peter's Denial

IN THE STEPS OF JESUS
After Jesus was arrested he was probably led up these stone steps, which date from the 1st century AD. They lead to the traditional site of Caiaphas' house.

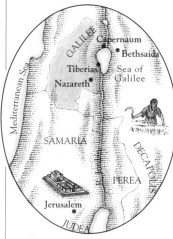

GALILEE
Jesus and all of his disciples, apart from Judas, came from Galilee, a province in the north of Palestine. Galileans spoke with a strong accent and were looked down on by the Judeans in the south.

Peter

Peter is asked three times if he knows Jesus, and three times he denies it

ARLIER, while on the Mount of Olives, Jesus had told his disciples that before the night was over, he would be betrayed by them. Peter had denied that this was possible, and Jesus had looked at him calmly, saying, "Before the cock crows at dawn, you will have disowned me three times." To this Peter had emphatically replied, "Never!"

Jesus was now under arrest, and was taken to the house of Caiaphas, the high priest. There, the scribes and elders and all the members of the Sanhedrin, the powerful Jewish council, had assembled and were waiting to interrogate him. Peter followed at a distance, watching to see what would happen. He went into the courtyard of Caiaphas' house and stood with the guards, who were warming themselves by the fire.

A servant girl came up to Peter and peered closely at him. "Were you not with Jesus of Galilee?" she asked him.

"I know no one of that name," said Peter, getting up and walking to the gateway.

A second girl approached him, saying to her companion, "This is one of the men who was with Jesus of Nazareth."

But Peter quickly denied it. "Not I," he said. "I swear I do not know the man."

By this time several people had gathered around, and were looking at him curiously. "Surely you are one of the disciples?" asked one. "You must be: you speak with a Galilean accent."

Peter turned on them angrily. "Have I not told you? I do not even know the man you are talking about!"

At these words a cock crowed and Peter suddenly remembered Jesus' words, foretelling how he would disown him. Peter walked out of the courtyard and broke down and wept.

The cock crows and Peter, remembering Jesus' words, goes out of the courtyard and weeps

COCK
Domesticated chickens were common in Palestine in Jesus' time. Cocks always crowed a few hours before dawn, and soldiers would use this as a signal to change the guard.

IMMEDIATELY THE COCK CREW. AND PETER REMEMBERED THE WORD OF JESUS, WHICH SAID UNTO HIM, "BEFORE THE COCK CROW, THOU SHALT DENY ME THRICE." AND HE WENT OUT, AND WEPT BITTERLY.
MATTHEW 26:74-75

Jesus Before the Sanhedrin

Jesus is brought before Caiaphas and the council of Jewish leaders

Caiaphas

Caiaphas and the council accuse Jesus of insulting God

ESUS WAS BROUGHT BEFORE Caiaphas the high priest and the council of Jewish leaders, the Sanhedrin. Determined to find him guilty, they questioned a number of men who had been bribed to lie about Jesus, but none could produce convincing evidence against the prisoner. Eventually, two came forward who swore they had heard Jesus say he could single-handedly destroy the temple, then magically rebuild it within three days.

"What do you say to this?" Caiaphas demanded. Jesus remained silent. Caiaphas spoke to him again. "Are you the Son of God?"

"I am," Jesus quietly replied.

Caiaphas leapt to his feet. "We need no more evidence!" he shouted triumphantly. "No man can be the Son of God! It is insulting God to say so, and the punishment for blasphemy is death!" At this, the members of the council crowded around Jesus, jeering and jostling him and spitting in his face.

The next morning, Jesus, bound and blindfolded, was taken to Pontius Pilate, the Roman governor of Judea.

AGAIN THE HIGH PRIEST ASKED HIM, AND SAID UNTO HIM, "ART THOU THE CHRIST, THE SON OF THE BLESSED?" AND JESUS SAID, "I AM."
MARK 14:61-62

Judas, full of remorse for having betrayed Jesus, goes away and hangs himself

When Judas heard what had happened, he was overcome with remorse. He went to the priests with the thirty pieces of silver they had given him. "I cannot keep your money for I have betrayed an innocent man," he said, throwing the silver onto the floor of the temple. Then in an agony of shame he went away and hanged himself.

The priests picked up the coins. "This is blood money: we cannot put it into the temple treasury." Having consulted with each other, they decided to spend the sum on the purchase of a certain field belonging to a potter. It would be used as a burying place for foreigners, and became known as the Field of Blood.

THIRTY SILVER PIECES
Above is a bronze coin box with Tyrian and Jewish silver shekels, the coinage that Judas may have been paid in. Thirty silver pieces, traditionally the price of a slave, was not worth a large amount in Jesus' time.

JUDAS TREE
The Judas tree, above, is the type of tree that is traditionally believed that Judas hanged himself on. No one knows why Judas betrayed Jesus. One idea is that Judas thought that Jesus was a political leader who had come to overthrow Roman rule and seize power for the Jewish people. When he realized he was mistaken, he betrayed Jesus.

The priests pick up the thirty pieces of silver that Judas had thrown down on the temple floor

Jesus Before Pilate

ESUS STOOD in the judgment hall before Pilate, the Roman governor, who questioned him closely. "Are you the king of the Jews?" he asked.

"It is as you say," Jesus replied.

To all other questions and charges Jesus remained silent, much to

PILATE'S COIN
Many new coins that were issued by Pontius Pilate, the Roman govenor of Judea, had a curved rod engraved on them, such as on the coin above. This was the symbol for a Roman augur, or fortune-teller, and replaced the Jewish symbols of palm branches and ears of wheat found on earlier coins. It was offensive to Jewish people, and showed Pilate's lack of sensitivity to Jewish feeling.

RITUAL WASHING
The bowl and jug shown above were found in a house in Pompeii, Italy, and date from Jesus' time. When Pilate washed his hands in front of the crowd, it symbolized that he wanted no part in condemning Jesus to death.

Pilate washes his hands in front of the people

Pilate gives the order for Barabbas to be released

He gives the order for Jesus to be flogged

Pilate's amazement. He could not find any fault with Jesus, and thought that the council had brought Jesus to him out of envy.

It was the custom during the Passover festival for one prisoner, chosen by the people, to be released. Pilate went out and asked the crowd who had gathered, "Whom do you wish me to set free, Barabbas, the rebel and murderer, or Jesus Christ?" He thought that with this choice, the people would ask for Jesus.

But the chief priests and councilors, determined that Jesus should die, persuaded the crowd to ask for Barabbas.

"Then," said Pilate, "what shall I do with Jesus, who is called 'King of the Jews'?"

"Crucify him!" came the cry.

"Why? What crime has he committed?"

But the crowd only shouted all the louder, "Crucify him!"

Pilate shrugged. He called for a bowl of water and publicly washed his hands, saying, "Take note that I am innocent of this man's blood." He gave the order for Barabbas to be released, then he had Jesus flogged before handing him over to the guard.

The soldiers took him to their quarters where they stripped him, dressed him in a robe of royal purple, and placed on his head a crown of thorns. Mockingly they knelt before him. "Hail, King of the Jews!" they jeered, beating him and spitting at him. When they tired of this, they dressed him again in his own clothes, then led him away to be executed in the Roman way, by crucifixion.

CROWN OF THORNS
Crowns were a symbol of royalty and honor in Jesus' time. The Roman soldiers wove a crown out of thorny branches and placed it on Jesus' head to mock the idea of Jesus as a king.

AND WHEN THEY HAD PLAITED A CROWN OF THORNS, THEY PUT IT UPON HIS HEAD, AND A REED IN HIS RIGHT HAND: AND THEY BOWED THE KNEE BEFORE HIM, AND MOCKED HIM, SAYING, "HAIL, KING OF THE JEWS!"
MATTHEW 27:29

The soldiers mockingly kneel before Jesus and shout "Hail King of the Jews!"

The Crucifixion

VIA DOLOROSA
Jesus is believed to have carried the cross along the Via Dolorosa, which means "way of sorrows." The route is marked by 14 "stations of the cross," which recall the events of Jesus' crucifixion.

A**S JESUS WAS LED AWAY** to be crucified, he was met by Simon of Cyrene. At once the guards seized Simon and forced him to help carry the cross. When they reached Calvary, one of the soldiers offered Jesus a drink of wine mixed with myrrh, but he turned away his head. Then they raised him on the cross, placing above him the mocking inscription, "Jesus of Nazareth, King of the Jews."

The guards threw lots for his clothes before sitting down to keep watch. As people passed to and fro, they taunted the man hanging from the cross. "If you are indeed the Son of God, why don't you save yourself?" they jeered. Then Jesus said, "Father, forgive them, for they do not know what they are doing."

Two robbers are crucified, one on either side of Jesus

Simon of Cyrene helps Jesus carry the cross

The guards throw lots for his clothes

THEN SAID JESUS, "FATHER, FORGIVE THEM; FOR THEY KNOW NOT WHAT THEY DO."
LUKE 23:34

Two robbers were crucified, one on either side of Jesus. One of the criminals hurled insults, but the other defended Jesus. Jesus said to this man, "Today, you will be with me in paradise."

At noon darkness fell on the land, a darkness which lasted until the third hour of the afternoon. Then Jesus cried aloud, "My God, my

God, why have you abandoned me?" Hearing him cry out, one of the men standing at the foot of the cross ran to fetch a sponge soaked in vinegar, which he put on the end of a pole and held up to Jesus' lips. Jesus cried out, "Father, into your hands I commend my spirit." Then his head fell lifeless on his breast. At that same moment, the curtain in the temple was ripped from top to bottom, and a tremor was felt in the very depths of the Earth.

One of the centurions who had been keeping guard said, "Truly this man was the Son of God." And many of the people who were near began to feel afraid. At a little distance stood several women who had come with Jesus from Galilee, among them Mary, his mother, Mary Magdalene, and Mary, the mother of James. They had no fear, and remained where they were, waiting.

That evening Joseph, a rich man from Arimathea, arrived. He was a member of the Jewish council and was one of Jesus' followers. He had come to ask Pilate if he might take down the body from the cross. Pilate gave his permission, so Joseph, helped by a man called Nicodemus, anointed Jesus' body with myrrh and aloes, and wrapped it in a sheet of clean linen. They then laid the body in an unused tomb cut in the rock.

WAS THIS CALVARY? Some people believe that the rocky hill above is the site of Calvary (Golgotha), whose name means "skull." One reason for this is that the rocks form the shape of a human skull. The hill became known as Gordon's Calvary, after a British general, Charles Gordon, who was convinced that this was where Jesus was crucified and buried.

Jesus' body is laid in a tomb

Several women remain near Jesus

Nicodemus

Joseph

Joseph and Nicodemus prepare Jesus' body for burial

AN ALTERNATIVE SITE The other possibility for the site of Calvary (Golgotha) is the low hill on which the Church of the Holy Sepulcher now stands, within the Old City of Jerusalem.

The Resurrection

Mary Magdalene tells Peter and John that Jesus' body has been taken from the tomb

John hesitates to go inside the tomb

Peter goes right into the tomb

BURIAL PLACE
The Bible says that Jesus' body was laid in a tomb cut out of rock, which was sealed with a large rolling stone. This type of tomb was common in Jesus' time. Jesus' body would have been laid along one of the rocky ledges that were cut into the walls inside the tomb. The round stone would have been rolled into position along a groove, and held over the entrance by a small stone.

EARLY IN THE MORNING while it was still dark, Mary Magdalene arrived at the tomb. She found to her astonishment that the stone had been rolled away from the entrance. The body was gone. She ran to Peter and also John, the disciple whom Jesus particularly loved. "They have taken the Lord from the tomb," she told them.

The two men hurried to the tomb. John ran ahead and reached it first, but hesitated to go inside. Then Peter arrived, and went right into the tomb. He saw the strips of linen and the burial cloth that had been wrapped around Jesus' head lying on the ground. John joined Peter inside the tomb. They both wondered if Jesus'body had been stolen or if he had risen from the dead.

Peter and John returned home, but Mary stayed by the tomb weeping. Suddenly she looked up to see two angels sitting where the body of Jesus had lain. "Why are you weeping?" they asked her.

"Because they have taken my Lord away."

As she spoke, she turned around and saw a man standing behind her in the shadows. It was Jesus, although at first Mary failed to recognize him. "Why are you weeping?" he said. Believing him to be the gardener, she asked him if he knew where the body had been taken.

"Mary, it is I!"

"My Lord!" she cried, her face full of joy.

"Go now," he told her. "Tell my friends that you have seen me, and that soon I will be with my Father in Heaven."

Mary ran back to tell the disciples the news. "With my own eyes I have seen the Lord!" she said.

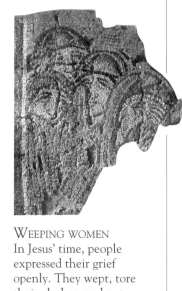

WEEPING WOMEN
In Jesus' time, people expressed their grief openly. They wept, tore their clothes, and put ashes on their heads.

Two angels are sitting inside the tomb

Mary turns around and sees Jesus standing behind her

On the Road to Emmaus

EMMAUS
No one knows the exact site of Emmaus, but some people think it was at the village of Amwas, shown above, which is about 20 miles (30 km) west of Jerusalem. The name "Emmaus" means "warm wells."

TWO OF JESUS' FORMER COMPANIONS were walking toward the village of Emmaus, discussing the tremendous events of the past days. As they went along, Jesus himself joined them, but neither man recognized him. "Why do you look so sad?" he asked them.

One of the two, Cleopas, gravely replied, "Where have you come from? Is it possible you have not heard the news?"

"What do you mean?" asked Jesus.

"We are sad because the great prophet, Jesus of Nazareth, has been crucified. We had believed him to be the saviour of our country, but when he died, all our hopes of salvation died with him."

"But do you not understand," said Jesus, "that Christ had to suffer first before he could be glorified?" And he explained what the prophets had foretold.

As they came near the village, the two companions persuaded him

Jesus

Cleopas

Jesus joins two companions who are traveling to Emmaus

When the friends realize that the stranger is Jesus, he disappears from their sight

DOUBTING THOMAS
This detail from a French illuminated manuscript shows Thomas looking at Jesus' wounds. Once Thomas had seen, he believed. Jesus said that a greater blessing awaits those who have faith without having seen him. Thomas' lack of belief earned him the name "Doubting Thomas."

to stay the night and to eat with them. As they sat at the table, Jesus broke the bread, blessed it, and gave some to his companions. As he did so, suddenly their eyes were opened and the friends knew who he was, but at the same moment that they recognized him, Jesus disappeared from their sight. The two men were amazed, and asked each other, "Did you not feel something wonderful when he was walking with us on the road, when he explained what the prophets had foretold?" They lost no time in hurrying back to Jerusalem to tell the disciples that they had seen their Lord.

As they were speaking, Jesus again came among them. "Peace be with you," he said. The disciples were terrified, convinced that they saw a ghost. "Why are you frightened?" Jesus asked them. "I am no ghost. Come, touch me. Look at me. Feel the wounds on my hands and feet. Ghosts do not have flesh and bones, as I have." Then he asked them for food, and they gave him some grilled fish, which he ate in front of them.

One of the disciples, Thomas, was not present on this occasion, but he was told later what had happened. He could not believe that it was the Lord whom the others had seen.

"Unless I can feel for myself the wounds on his body I cannot accept that this man is Christ," he said.

A week later the disciples were together, Thomas with them, when Jesus entered.

"Thomas," said Jesus, "put your fingers on my side, touch the holes in my hands. Stop doubting and believe."

"My Lord and my God," said Thomas.

Jesus replied, "You believe because you have seen with your own eyes, but more blessed are those who have not seen and yet still believe."

Jesus tells Thomas to touch the wound in his side and the holes in his hands

The Ascension

At Jesus' bidding, the disciples let down their nets, and find them heavy with fish

Peter swims to the shore to see Jesus

CHRISTIAN SYMBOL
The fish was an early Christian symbol. It was used because the Greek word for fish is made up of the first letter of each word of the Greek phrase, "Jesus Christ, God's Son, Saviour."

NE NIGHT several of the disciples, including Peter, Thomas, James, and John, went out fishing on the Sea of Galilee. All night they fished, but caught nothing. As dawn broke, Jesus, unrecognized, stood watching them on the shore nearby.

"Have you caught anything, my friends?" he called to them.

"Nothing," they tiredly replied.

"Let down your nets on the right side of the boat," he told them. And when they did so, they found the nets so heavy with fish they were barely able to pull them up.

At this sign John said to Peter, "It is the Lord." At once Peter threw

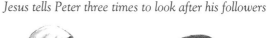

Jesus tells Peter three times to look after his followers

ASCENSION
Jesus ascended to Heaven, as shown in this stone carving, 40 days after he rose from the dead.

off his coat, leapt into the water, and began swimming for the shore. The others followed by boat, dragging their laden nets behind them.

Once on land, they saw fish cooking over a fire. "Come and eat," said Jesus. This was the third time that the Lord had appeared to his disciples since he had risen from the dead.

After they had eaten, Jesus turned to Peter. "Do you love me and have faith in me?"

"Yes, Lord," Peter replied.

"Then look after my flock, my followers."

Again Jesus said, "Do you love me?"

Peter answered, "Yes, Lord, you know that I love you."

"Look after my flock."

A third time Jesus said, "Peter, do you truly love me?"

This time Peter felt hurt that Jesus did not seem to believe him. "Lord, you know everything. You know that I love you."

"Take care of my flock."

Later, Jesus spoke to all of the disciples, telling them that once he had left them they would receive power from the Holy Spirit to help them spread the word of God throughout the world.

After he had spoken, Jesus was lifted up out of their sight, hidden from them in a cloud. As the disciples stood gazing up into the sky, two men dressed in white appeared beside them. "Jesus, who has been taken up into Heaven, will one day return to you in the same way."

Two men dressed in white appear beside the disciples

Jesus is lifted up out of the disciples' sight, hidden from them in a cloud

Tongues of Fire

SUDDENLY THERE CAME A SOUND
FROM HEAVEN AS OF A RUSHING
MIGHTY WIND, AND IT FILLED ALL
THE HOUSE WHERE THEY WERE
SITTING. AND THERE APPEARED
UNTO THEM CLOVEN TONGUES
LIKE AS OF FIRE, AND IT SAT
UPON EACH OF THEM.
ACTS OF THE APOSTLES 2:2-3

*A small flame flickers
over the head of each
apostle, a sign that the
Holy Spirit is with them*

THE DISCIPLES, as they continued in their work of spreading God's word, also became known as the apostles. In order to replace the traitor Judas, and bring their number again up to twelve, they put forward the names of two men, Joseph and Matthias. Having prayed for guidance, they all cast lots, and in this way Matthias was chosen.

Later, on the day of the Jewish harvest festival of Pentecost, the apostles were gathered in one room. Suddenly the sound of a mighty wind was heard rushing through the house, and over the head of each man flickered a small flame, a sign that the Holy Spirit was with them. As they turned in amazement and began to talk, they found they were able to speak in many different languages.

As the disciples walked through the streets of Jerusalem, news of their astonishing gift spread far and wide. Jewish people from many different countries had come to stay in Jerusalem for Pentecost. They came up to talk with the apostles, and were amazed because the apostles could speak and understand any language from any part of the world.

Eventually Peter started to preach to the crowd. He told them of Jesus of Nazareth and the miracles worked by him in God's name, and how Jesus had died on the cross and then rose from the dead, and was now in Heaven by God's right hand.

"But what should we do? How shall we be saved?" everyone anxiously asked one another.

"Turn away from sin," said Peter. "Repent and be baptized in the name of Jesus Christ and you will receive the gift of the Holy Spirit. This promise is for you and your children." Those who accepted what Peter said were baptized: about three thousand became followers of Jesus that day.

DIASPORA
Throughout much of their history, many Jewish people have lived in countries far from Judea. This is called the "Diaspora," a Greek word meaning "scattering." By the 1st century AD many Jewish people had settled in other countries, such as Italy and Egypt. Jerusalem was still thought of as the center of Jewish faith, and the Bible says that Jewish people came from many lands to celebrate the festival of Pentecost in the holy city.

Peter preaches to the crowd

Peter the Healer

Peter   John

*Peter tells the beggar
to get up and walk*

NE AFTERNOON Peter and John went to the temple to pray. Outside the gateway called Beautiful was a lame man who had been unable to walk from birth, and now begged for coins from passers-by. As the two apostles came toward him, he asked them for money. "Look at me," said Peter, holding out his hand to the beggar. "I do not have silver and gold, but what I have I give to you. In the name of Jesus of Nazareth, get up and walk!" At once the man leapt to his feet, and without any support went with Peter and John into the temple courtyard. He was overjoyed that he had been healed, and loudly sang songs of praise to God.

People were astonished to see the beggar walk, and soon a crowd had gathered around the three men. "Why are you amazed?" Peter asked them. "This is not our doing. It is by faith in Jesus that this man was made strong." Then Peter began to speak to the crowd about Jesus.

The priests and Sadducees and the captain of the temple guard were

THE WESTERN WALL
Above is a section of the Western Wall, the only remaining part of Herod's Temple. Jews come here to pray and to mourn the destruction of Jerusalem in AD 70. They tuck written prayers and requests in between the huge blocks of stone that make up the wall.

A crowd gathers around Peter, John, and the beggar, and Peter begins to preach

Peter   beggar   John

The priests and the Sadducees are angry

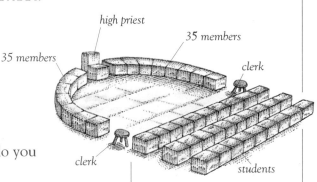

angry that Jesus' followers were preaching to the
people. They had Peter and John arrested and
thrown into jail.

The next day the prisoners were brought before the
Jewish council, the Sanhedrin. "By whose authority do you
preach in the temple?" the judges asked them.

Inspired by the Holy Spirit, Peter replied, "It is of Jesus of Nazareth
that I preach, and through him that the lame man was healed."

*Peter and John are arrested and
brought before the Sanhedrin*

SANHEDRIN
The Sanhedrin, or
council, was the highest
court of justice among
the Jewish people in
Jesus' time. Its 71
members sat in a semi-
circle, with the high
priest – the leader of the
council – in the middle.
Two clerks sat on stools
and took notes during
meetings. The Sanhedrin
was dominated by the
Sadducees, who were a
powerful group made up
of priests and wealthy
people. The other
members included
Pharisees, who were
upholders of the Jewish
law, and scribes, who
were writers and
specialists in the law.
The Sanhedrin had the
power to judge, punish,
and imprison the Jewish
people, but only the
Romans could pass the
death penalty.

When the council saw that the apostles were simple, uneducated
men, they were astonished, and took note that these men had been
friends of Jesus. They ordered Peter and John to leave, then discussed
among themselves what they should do. They knew they could not
deny that a miracle had happened, but they did not want the news
spreading any farther. So they called the two men back and warned
them not to preach in the name of Jesus any more. To this Peter and
John replied, "Judge for yourselves whether it is right in God's eyes to
obey you rather than God. We cannot help but speak of all we have
seen and heard." The Sanhedrin could not decide how to punish
them, so they reluctantly let them go.

AND THEY CALLED THEM, AND
COMMANDED THEM NOT TO
SPEAK AT ALL NOR TEACH IN
THE NAME OF JESUS.
**ACTS OF THE APOSTLES
4:18**

Saul's Journey to Damascus

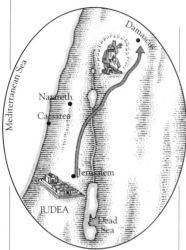

AS HE JOURNEYED, HE CAME NEAR DAMASCUS: AND SUDDENLY THERE SHINED ROUND ABOUT HIM A LIGHT FROM HEAVEN: AND HE FELL TO THE EARTH, AND HEARD A VOICE SAYING UNTO HIM, "SAUL, SAUL, WHY PERSECUTEST THOU ME?"
ACTS OF THE APOSTLES 9:3-4

SAUL WAS ONE OF the great enemies of the early church. Due to leave Jerusalem for Damascus, he went to see the high priest and obtained from him the authority to have any man or woman arrested whom he suspected of being a follower of Jesus.

As he approached the city of Damascus, Saul was suddenly surrounded by a blinding white light. He staggered, and fell to the ground. Then a voice spoke in his ear. "Saul, Saul, why do you persecute me?"

Trembling and astonished, Saul said, "Who are you, Lord?"

And he heard the voice say, "I am Jesus, whom you are persecuting. Rise and go into the city and there you will be told what you must do."

Unsteadily, Saul got to his feet, but when he opened his eyes, he found he was unable to see. His companions led him into the city, and for three days he remained sightless, refusing both food and drink.

On the way to Damascus, Saul is blinded by a white light and falls to the ground

Saul's sight is restored by Ananias

There lived in Damascus a disciple of Jesus called Ananias, and to him the Lord appeared in a vision. "Go to the house of Judas in Straight Street, and ask there for Saul of Tarsus. You must lay your hands on him and restore his sight, for I have chosen him to do great things for my people."

Ananias did as he had been instructed and went to Judas' house. "Brother," said Ananias to Saul, "the Lord has sent me so that you may see again and be filled with the Holy Spirit." He then laid his hands gently over Saul's eyes. Immediately his sight returned. Saul joyfully rose from his bed and was baptized. For the next few days he remained in Damascus to preach in the synagogues and spread the word of God. All who heard him were amazed at such a change of heart. "Is it possible," they asked each other, "that this is the same man who so fiercely persecuted the followers of Jesus?"

Some people, however, saw him as an enemy and planned to kill him. Saul heard of their plan, and with the help of some of the disciples he escaped at night in a basket lowered over the city wall. He then made his way to Jerusalem. At first, the disciples there were afraid of Saul and refused to accept him.

Saul escapes at night from Damascus in a basket lowered over the city wall

However, one of their number, Barnabas, believed Saul, and taking him to the apostles, explained what had happened on the road to Damascus. After this, Saul was welcomed as a true follower of Jesus.

STRAIGHT STREET
Above is Straight Street in Damascus, where Saul's sight was restored. It was one of the main routes through Damascus, a major trading center. It is called "straight" because it runs in a straight line through the city.

FROM SAUL TO PAUL
After Saul was converted, he became known by his Roman name, Paul. Shown in the mosaic above, Paul was a clear speaker and writer and played a vital role in the development of Christianity.

Peter and Cornelius

THERE LIVED IN CAESAREA a centurion called Cornelius, a good man who worshiped God and was generous to the poor. One day an angel appeared to him. "You must send men to Joppa to bring back Peter," said the angel. "He is lodging there with Simon, a tanner, in a house by the sea."

Once the angel had gone, Cornelius called two of his servants and a trusted soldier and sent them to Joppa.

The following day about noon, when Cornelius' men were approaching the city, Peter went up to the roof to pray. He was hungry, but while waiting for food to be prepared, he fell into a trance. He saw Heaven opening above him, and a great sheet descending to the Earth containing every sort of animal and bird. "Eat, Peter, eat," said a voice.

"Surely not Lord, I have never eaten anything that is unclean," Peter replied.

"Nothing is unclean that God has made clean," said the voice. Two more times Peter saw the same vision before the sheet was taken back to Heaven.

Cornelius is a good man who is generous to the poor

TANNER'S TOOLS
A tanner made leather from animal skins. He scraped hair and fat from the skins using a tool made of bone, like the ones above. He soaked the skins in lime and the juices of plants to soften them. The bad smell their work produced meant that tanners lived outside the towns and cities.

Peter is on the roof of Simon's house when he sees a great sheet descending containing every sort of animal and bird

Cornelius' men come to the house to ask Peter to return with them

Peter

Cornelius

*As Peter enters the house, Cornelius
falls down on his knees before him*

JOPPA
Joppa, modern-day
Jaffa, lies on the
Mediterranean Sea and is
one of the oldest seaports
in the world. It is
mentioned in both the
Old and New
Testaments. This
attractive city, whose
name means "beautiful,"
is built on a rocky hill
about 116 ft (35 m) high.
It was once the main port
for Jerusalem, 35 miles
(56 km) away. Today,
only small fishing boats
use the port.

Peter was puzzling over the meaning of the vision when the three
men sent by Cornelius arrived at Simon's house, where they were
invited to stay as guests.

The next day, Peter, understanding that it was God's will, returned
with them to Caesarea. Cornelius, who was surrounded by his family
and friends, was waiting to greet him. As Peter entered the house, he
fell down on his knees before him. "Do not kneel," said Peter gently.
"I, too, am a man, just as you are."

Peter then spoke to all who were gathered there. "God has shown
me that all people, Jew and Gentile, are equal in his eyes, that none
should be regarded as inferior or unclean."

After a few days Peter went on to Jerusalem. The apostles and other
followers of Jesus criticized him for mixing with people of different
beliefs, with Gentiles who had not been baptized. Peter told them of
his vision. "All people are the same in the sight of God," he said.

AND AS PETER WAS COMING
IN, CORNELIUS MET HIM, AND
FELL DOWN AT HIS FEET, AND
WORSHIPED HIM. BUT PETER
TOOK HIM UP, SAYING, "STAND
UP; I MYSELF ALSO AM A MAN."
**ACTS OF THE APOSTLES
10:25-26**

Peter in Prison

After the angel has led him out of prison, Peter finds himself alone in the city

Peter lies sleeping in prison, chained to two soldiers

An angel appears and tells Peter to get up quickly

AND, BEHOLD, THE ANGEL OF THE LORD CAME UPON HIM, AND A LIGHT SHINED IN THE PRISON: AND HE SMOTE PETER ON THE SIDE, AND RAISED HIM UP, SAYING, "ARISE UP QUICKLY." AND HIS CHAINS FELL OFF FROM HIS HANDS.
ACTS OF THE APOSTLES 12:7

KING HEROD AGRIPPA was a fierce enemy of the church. Having had several Christians executed, he arrested Peter during the Passover festival and threw him into prison. There he was heavily guarded throughout the four watches of the day and night by four squads of four soldiers each.

The night before his trial, Peter was sleeping, bound with two chains between two of the soldiers, while the remaining two stood guard at the door. Suddenly an angel appeared in a blaze of light and struck Peter on his side. "Get up quickly," he said. "Put on your cloak and sandals and follow me." As he spoke, Peter's chains fell away and he was free. As if in a dream, Peter followed the angel out of the prison. Silently, they passed the guards, and the gates of the prison opened as of their own accord.

Once out into the streets of the city, the angel disappeared and Peter found himself alone. Now he knew that this had not been a dream, but that God had rescued him from imprisonment and from King Herod's evil plans.

Rhoda

Peter went straight to the house of Mary, mother of Mark, where a number of people had gathered to pray for him. His knock was heard by Rhoda, a young servant girl. But when she heard Peter's voice, she was so overjoyed that instead of opening the door she ran back and told the company who it was standing outside. "It cannot be!" they exclaimed. "He is in prison: it cannot be him!

But Rhoda insisted that it was Peter at the door, so that they began to wonder if it could be his ghost. Peter kept on knocking until at last they went to open the door. When they saw it was indeed Peter, they were astonished.

Rhoda, a young servant girl, hears Peter's voice at the door and runs to tell everyone in the house

The next morning panic broke out in the prison when it was discovered that Peter was gone. Herod was beside himself with rage and organized a thorough search, but Peter was nowhere to be found. No one could explain what had happened, and in his fury Herod commanded that all Peter's guards be put to death.

The people are astonished when they open the door and see Peter standing there

ANGELS
In the Bible, angels are spiritual beings who are close to God and are immortal. Traditionally, angels were often depicted as having wings, similar to the angel in this stained-glass panel. Angels fulfilled a number of roles. They were sent by God as messengers of good news. They guided, instructed, and warned people. They were protectors – helping people in times of need. They carried out God's judgment. They praised God and obeyed him at all times.

Paul's Journeys

Paul traveled to see new groups of Christians.

Aᴛᴛᴇʀ Pᴀᴜʟ ʙᴇᴄᴀᴍᴇ a Christian, he traveled widely to spread the word about Jesus. He used the network of roads that the Romans had built throughout their empire. Paul was a Roman citizen and this gave him freedom of movement and some protection on his journeys. The fastest way to travel was on horseback and by ship, which was how letters were carried from place to place. When Paul could not be with new groups of Christians, he wrote letters to them about following Jesus.

Paul's First Journey

Paul traveled around the eastern part of the Mediterranean Sea to spread the message of Christianity. On his first journey he went to the island of Cyprus, where his companion Barnabas was born. They taught in the synagogues at Salamis and in other parts of the island. When they returned to the mainland they were welcomed in some places, but at others, such as Iconium and Lystra, the people refused to listen to their message.

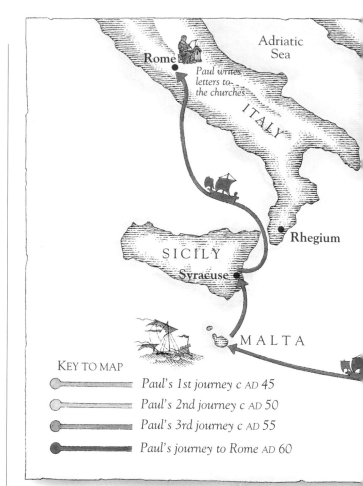

The map above shows the routes of Paul's three missionary journeys and his final journey to Rome.

KEY TO MAP

Paul's 1st journey c AD 45
Paul's 2nd journey c AD 50
Paul's 3rd journey c AD 55
Paul's journey to Rome AD 60

Cʏᴘʀᴜs
On his first journey Paul visited Cyprus, a beautiful Mediterranean island with a rocky coastline. A Jewish community had been on the island since the 4th century ʙᴄ, and even before Paul arrived, there were some Christians living there. The purpose of Paul's journeys was to help more people become Christians, as well as to support and encourage those who had already become followers of Jesus.

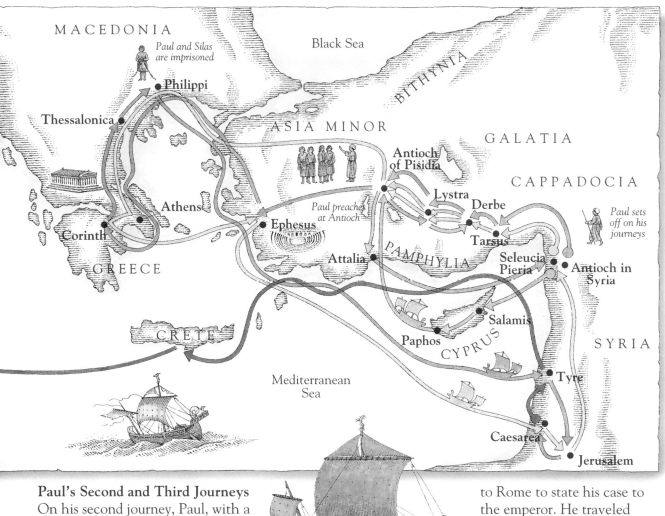

MACEDONIA

Paul and Silas are imprisoned

Philippi

Thessalonica

Black Sea

BITHYNIA

ASIA MINOR

GALATIA

Antioch of Pisidia

CAPPADOCIA

Lystra

Derbe

Paul preaches at Antioch

Athens

Ephesus

Paul sets off on his journeys

Tarsus

Corinth

GREECE

Attalia

PAMPHYLIA

Seleucia Pieria

Antioch in Syria

Salamis

Paphos

CYPRUS

SYRIA

CRETE

Mediterranean Sea

Tyre

Caesarea

Jerusalem

Paul's Second and Third Journeys

On his second journey, Paul, with a friend named Silas, traveled farther afield. He preached in the great cities of Philippi, Ephesus, and Athens and Corinth in Greece. On his third missionary journey, Paul stayed for some time at Ephesus. Travelers from east and west came by land and sea to this great city. In the massive theater a huge crowd demonstrated against Paul when he tried to prevent the worship of the goddess Artemis, who was called Diana by the Romans.

Grain ship

Paul's Last Journey

Paul was arrested when he returned to Jerusalem to care for the Christians there. His last long journey took place because he asked to be taken

to Rome to state his case to the emperor. He traveled under guard on a grain ship, that was wrecked off the coast of Malta. When they eventually reached Rome, Paul was put under house arrest.

During his imprisonment, he wrote many letters of encouragement to the Christian churches he had helped establish.

We do not know when and how Paul died, but it is thought that he may have been beheaded on the orders of the Emperor Nero in the year AD 64. In the 30 years between his conversion and his death, Paul founded churches in 20 cities of the Roman Empire.

Nero was emperor from AD 54-68.

Paul's Journey to Rome

Paul is shipwrecked off the coast of Malta

IT WAS FINALLY DECIDED that Paul should be taken to Rome and stand trial before Caesar himself. He and certain other prisoners were put in the charge of a centurion named Julius, and under his care they set sail from Adramyttium.

As they came near to the island of Crete, a strong wind began to blow, and soon a storm was howling round them. In fear of their lives, the sailors hauled down the sails, then strengthened the sides of the ship with ropes before finally throwing overboard anything they could lay their hands on. For three days and nights the storm raged and death seemed near.

Paul, however, calmed their fears. "God has told me that although the ship will be wrecked, none of you will die," he said to them. Eventually the watch reported that they were running into shallow water. Paul repeated that they need not fear, that no harm would come to any of them. "Now you must eat," he said, "to keep up your strength and your spirits. Remember what I have told you: no one will lose his life, but you must have food to survive." Then Paul took some bread, broke it into pieces, and gave thanks to God. Everyone drew courage from this and began to eat.

At dawn they saw that they had drifted near the shore, and so by hoisting the mainsail they brought the ship onto a sandy bank

AND WHEN NEITHER SUN NOR STARS IN MANY DAYS APPEARED, AND NO SMALL TEMPEST LAY ON US, ALL HOPE THAT WE SHOULD BE SAVED WAS THEN TAKEN AWAY.
ACTS OF THE APOSTLES 27:20

Paul is bitten by a viper, but is unharmed

where she ran aground before breaking up in the rough water. At first the soldiers wanted to kill the prisoners, fearing that they might in the confusion try to escape. Julius, however, anxious for Paul's safety, persuaded them to let the captives save themselves as best they could. He ordered all who could swim to jump into the sea, the rest to hang on to any broken plank or piece of rigging and propel themselves to land.

Paul cures Publius' father

The island to which they had come was Malta, and the inhabitants welcomed the shipwrecked survivors, lighting a fire to warm them, for it was raining and bitterly cold. Paul, who had been gathering sticks for the fire, was suddenly attacked by a viper, whose poisonous bite is known to be fatal.

But Paul, unhurt, shook off the snake, which left not even a mark on his hand. The people were amazed. "This man must be a god," they said.

The governor of the island, Publius, gave them all lodging in his own quarters. Publius' father was dangerously ill with a fever, and Paul cured the sick man by laying his hands on him. After this, many others came to him to be healed, and Paul was treated with the greatest honor and respect.

Eventually they left Malta and sailed to Rome, where Paul and the other prisoners were handed over to the captain of the guard. Paul was allowed to live comfortably in his own rented house, but with a sentry to watch him day and night. Many came to hear him, and for two years Paul welcomed all comers, explaining the teaching of Jesus and spreading the word of God.

ST. PAUL'S BAY
Above is St. Paul's Bay, in Malta, where Paul is believed to have been shipwrecked. Paul's voyage took place in winter, when storms are most likely to arise on the Mediterranean Sea. In the Bible it says that as the ship approached Malta, it struck a sand bank. This detail fits St. Paul's Bay, which has a sandy ridge that runs out into the sea.

Paul leaves Malta and sets sail for Rome

Index

A

aloes, 25
Ananias, 53
angels, 42-43, 56-57
anointment, 26, 41
Antioch, 59
apostles, 7; *see also* disciples
Artemis, 59

B

baptism, 49
Barabbas, 39
barley, 18
Barnabas, 53, 58
Beersheba, Map on title page
Bethany, Map on title page, 24
Bethlehem, Map on title page
Bethsaida, Map on title page, 18
bread, 18, 30; making, 24
burial, 25

C

Caesarea, Map on title page, 59
Caesarea Philippi, 22
Caiaphas, 27, 35, 36
Calvary, 40, 41
Cana (Kefar Kana), 8, 9
Capernaum, Map on title page, 10, 12
Carmel, Mount, Map on title page
centurion, 13
Christians/Christianity, 7, 46, 58
Cleopas, 44
Coenaculum, 28
coins, 38, *see also* silver
Corinth, 59
Cornelius, 54-55
council, 36, 51
cross, 7, 40
crown of thorns, 39
Cyprus, 58

D

Damascus, Map on title page, 52, 53
Dead Sea, Map on title page
demons, 15

D (continued)

Devil, *see* Satan
Diana, 59
Diaspora, 49
disciples, 7, 14, 18, 20-21, 28-29, 30-31, 32-33, 45, 46-47, 48-49; *see also* apostles
Doubting Thomas, 45

E

Ebal, Mount, Map on title page
Elijah, and transfiguration of Jesus, 22-23
Emmaus, Map on title page, 44
Ephesus, 59
Epistles, *see* letters

F

Field of Blood, 37
fire, tongues of, 48-49
fish, as Christian symbol, 46
foot bath, 29

G

Gadara, Map on title page
Gadarenes, 15
Galilee, Map on title page, 6, 34; Sea of 6, 7, 14, 20
Gaza, Map on title page
Gennesaret, Lake of, 7
Gethsemane, Garden of, 32-33
Golgotha, *see* Calvary
Gordon, Charles, 41
Gospels, see John, Mark, Matthew

H

harp, 9
Hebron, Map on title page
Hermon, Mount, 23
Herod, Agrippa, 56, 57
Holy City, *see* Jerusalem
Holy Spirit, 47, 49
houses, 11

J

James, brother of John, 17, 22, 32, 46
Jericho, Map on title page
Jerusalem, Map on title page; *see also* Jesus
Jesus, 6-7; transfiguration of, 22-23; and Mary, Martha, and Lazarus, 24-25, 26-27; and the disciples, 28-29; and the Last Supper, 30-31; in the Garden of Gethsemane, 32-33; under arrest, 35, 36-37, 38-39; Crucifixion of, 40-41; Resurrection of, 42-43; on the road to Emmaus, 44-45; Ascension, of 46-47; see also miracles
Jewish people, 49; and Diaspora, 49
John, 17, 22, 28, 31, 32, 42, 46, 50-51; Gospel of, 31
Joppa (Jaffa), Map on title page 55
Jordan, River, Map on title page
Joseph of Arimathea, 7, 41
Judea, map on title page
Judeans, *see* Jewish people
Judas Iscariot, 26-27, 31, 33, 37
Judas tree, 37
Julius, 60-61

K

Kingdom of Heaven, 22; keys of, 22

L

Last Supper, the, 30-31
Lazarus, 7, 24-25, 26-27
Legion, 15
lepers/leprosy, 10
letters, by Paul, 58, 59
Lystra, 58

M

Magdala, 6
Malta, 59, 61
Mark, 33; Gospel, 33
Martha, 7, 24-25, 26-27
Mary, mother of James, 7, 41

Mary, Mother of Jesus; and birth/childhood of Jesus, 7; and marriage feast of Cana, 8; and the Crucifixion, 41

Mary, sister of Martha, 7, 24-25, 26-27

Mary of Magdala (Mary Magdalene), 7, 41, 42

Matthew, 7

Matthias, 49

Messiah, 7

miracles: calming the storm, 14; the centurion's servant, 12-13; feeding of the five thousand, 18-19; the Gadarene swine, 15; healing the sick, 10-11, 16; Jairus' daughter, 16-17; the marriage feast of Cana, 8-9; walking on the water, 20-21

money, 38

Moses, and transfiguration of Jesus, 22-23

Mount of Beatitudes, Map on title page

Mount Carmel, Map on title page

Mount Ebal, Map on title page

Mount Hermon, 23

Mount of Olives, 32

Mount Tabor, Map on title page

mourning, 17

music, 9, 17

myrrh, 25

N

Nazareth, Map on title page, 6

Nero, Emperor, 59

Nicodemus, 41

O

olive tree, 32

Olives, Mount of, 32

P

Passover, Feast of, 28

Paul, 52-53, 58-59, 60-61; see also Saul

Perea, Map on title page

Peter, 16, 21, 22, 28, 29, 31, 32, 33, 34-35, 49, 50, 51; and the Resurrection, 42; and the Ascension, 46-47; and Cornelius, 54-55; in prison, 56-57

Pharisees, 11, 51

pigs, 15

pipes, 9, 17

Pontius Pilate, Map on title page 36, 38-39, 41

Publius, 61

R

Rhoda, 57

ritual washing, 38

roads, Roman, 58

Romans, 13, 51

Rome, Paul in, 58, 59, 61

roofs, 11

rooster, 35

S

Sabbath, 6

Sadducees, 50, 51

Samaria, Map on title page

Sanhedrin, 27, 35, 36-37, 51

Satan, 15

Saul, 52-53; see also Paul

scribes, 51

Sea of Galilee, 6, 7, 14, 20

Silas, 59

silver, thirty pieces of, 27, 37

Simon the Cyrene, 40

Simon Peter, see Peter

Son of God, 7, 22, 23, 36

spikenard plant, 26

St. Paul's Bay, Malta, 61

synagogue, 16

T

Tabor, Mount, Map on title page

tambourine, 9

tanner, 54

thirty pieces of silver, 27, 37

Thomas, 45

Tiberias, Map on title page Sea of, 7

tomb, 42

transfiguration, 22-23

trees: Judas tree, 37; olive, 32

V

Via Dolorosa, 40

W

water carrier/jars, 8

weddings, 8

Western Wall, 50

wine, 8, 30

Who's Who in the Bible Stories

ANANIAS The Christian who restored Saul's sight. *Page 53*

BARABBAS The criminal who was set free instead of Jesus. *Page 39*

BARNABAS A Christian from Cyprus who briefly traveled with Paul. *Page 53, 58*

CAIAPHAS The high priest at the time of Jesus' arrest and crucifixion. *Pages 27, 35, 36*

CLEOPAS One of the two men who met Jesus on the road to Emmaus. *Page 44*

CORNELIUS The Roman centurion whom Peter visited. *Pages 54-55*

ELIJAH A great prophet of Israel who had a contest with the priests of Baal. *Pages 22-23*

HEROD AGRIPPA A fierce enemy of the early church. *Pages 56-57*

JAIRUS The leader of the synagogue whose daughter Jesus healed. *Pages 16-17*

JAMES The name of two of the 12 disciples. *Pages 17, 22, 32, 46*

JESUS CHRIST Regarded by Christians as the Son of God, and the Messiah predicted in the Old Testament. The main focus of Christian faith and the central figure in the New Testament. *Pages 6-47*

JOHN One of the 12 disciples, the brother of James. He wrote the fourth Gospel. *Pages 17, 22, 28, 31, 32, 42, 46, 50-51, 62-65*

JOSEPH One of the men put forward to replace Judas. *Page 49*

JOSEPH OF ARIMATHEA

The man who provided a tomb for Jesus' body. *Pages 7, 41*

JUDAS ISCARIOT The disciple who betrayed Jesus. *Pages 26-27, 31, 33, 37*

JULIUS The centurion who escorted Paul on the journey to Rome. *Pages 60-61*

LAZARUS The brother of Mary and Martha. Jesus raised him from the dead. *Pages 7, 24-25, 26-27*

MARK The writer of one of the four Gospels. His mother's house in Jerusalem was a meeting place for the early Church. *Page 33*

MARTHA The sister of Lazarus and Mary, and close friend of Jesus. *Pages 7, 24-24, 26-27*

MARY The mother of Jesus. *Pages 8, 41*

MARY The sister of Martha and Lazarus, and close friend of Jesus. *Pages 7, 24-25, 26-27*

MARY The mother of the disciple James. *Page 41*

MARY MAGDALENE The first witness of the resurrection. *Pages 24-25, 26-27*

MATTHEW A tax collector who became one of the 12 disciples. The writer of one of the Gospels. *Page 7*

MATTHIAS He became one of the 12 disciples after the death of Judas Iscariot. *Page 49*

MOSES The man who led the Israelites out of Egypt to search for the promised land. *Pages 22-23*

NERO Roman Emperor before whom Paul stood trial. *Page 59*

NICODEMUS The Jewish leader who helped prepare Jesus' body for burial. *Page 41*

PAUL/SAUL At first a persecutor of Christians, he became one of the greatest Christian leaders after he saw a vision of Jesus. In his travels he helped build up the early Church. *Pages 52-53, 58-61*

PETER A fisherman who became one of the 12 disciples and a close friend of Jesus. *Pages 16, 21, 22, 28-35, 42, 46-47 49-51, 54-57*

PONTIUS PILATE The Roman governor who ordered the crucifixion of Jesus. Map on title page; *pages 36, 38-39, 41*

PUBLIUS The governor of Malta whose father Paul healed. *Page 61*

RHODA An early Christian who answered the door to Peter after he had escaped from prison. *Page 57*

SATAN The name sometimes given to the Devil, who is thought to be the source of all sin and evil. *Page 15*

SAUL The first king of Israel. *Pages 52-53*

SAUL see PAUL

SILAS He traveled with Paul on some of his missionary journeys. *Page 59*

SIMON The tanner at whose house Peter had a vision. *Pages 54-55*

SIMON OF CYRENE The man from Cyrene who carried Jesus' cross. *Page 40*

THOMAS One of the 12 disciples. He doubted at first that Jesus had risen from the dead. *Page 45*

Acknowledgments

Photographic Credits
l=left, r=right, t=top, c=center, b=bottom

ASAP:/Mike Ganon 8tl /Avi Hirshfield 35tr/Garo Nalbandian 11tr, 20bl, 34tl, 41tr, 44tl.
Trustees of the British Museum: 59br.
DAS/Jamie Simpson 40tl.
E.T.Archive: 46bl.
Chris Fairclough: 50c.
Werner Forman Archive; 31br.

Giraudon: 45tr Musée Condé, Chantilly.
Sonia Halliday: 6b, 22bl, 23tr, 28bl, 33tr, 53br, 57cr.
Robert Harding Picture Library: 13tr, 58bl.wLise Dennis 41br/T.Jacobi 24tl.
Erich Lessing Archive: 10tl, 42bl.
Magnum:/René Burri 7c.
Zev Radovan: 9tr, 26bl, 32bl, 38tl, 54cl.
R.M.N; 15br Louvre.
Scala: 38bl Museo Nazionale Naples.
Zefa: 32tl, 37cr, 55tr, 61tr.

DK would like to thank:
Tim Ridley, Nick Goodall and

Gary Ombler at the DK Studio; Dorian Spencer Davies; Antonio Forcione; Christopher Gillingwater; Polly Goodman; George Hart; Alan Hills; James W. Hunter; Robin Hunter; Marcus James; Anna Kunst; Michelle de Larrabeiti; Antonio Montoro; Anderley Moore; Jackie Ogburn; Derek Peach; Lenore Person; Dino Politis; Lara Tankel Holtz and Martin Wilson for their help in producing this book.

Picture research by: Diana Morris
Index by: Lynn Bresler